A SALAD Soiree

Eclectic Recipes for Everyone

Ashley Kipp

Photography and design by Marc Kipp

For my parents.
Thank you for always inspiring me.

Table of Contents

Foreward *7*

Starters and Sides
Citrus Punch *11*
Dijon Potatoes *12*
Fiery Red *13*
Dinner Flowers *15*
Fresh Mediterranean *16*
Grilled Vegetable *17*
Fantastic Feta *19*
Grapefruit Avocado Dijon *20*
Holiday Greens *22*
The Native *25*
Pico de Gallo *26*
Rasparagus *27*
Sweet and Tangy Mediterranean *28*

Main Meals
Citrus Basil Fish *32*
Everything but the Kitchen Sink *33*
Island Beef *34*
Pure Energy *35*
"Rawsta" Fresca *37*
Shining Mountain Waldorf *38*
Simple Grilled Chicken *39*
Spicy Peach Chicken *40*

The Sweeter Side
Berry Fruity *45*
Strawberry Ricotta *47*
Muesli Fruit *48*
Winter Wheat Berry *49*

Foreword

Growing up, I was very fortunate to have parents who instilled in me a true appreciation for good food. As a daughter of two gourmet food brokers, I was constantly exposed to the flavors of the world, and to the chefs who worked with those flavors each in their own unique way. I watched and learned from the very best. Often times the lessons I learned involved creating simple and exotic recipes from whatever was lurking about in the cupboard; nothing special required. Still, the main idea, I learned through the years, was to be creative, but to always create the very best.

As a result, I am ingrained with the desire to use and create wonderful food. Even when things are tight, my upbringing has taught me to never, ever skimp on food. Not only is good food our nourishment and sustenance physically, it also serves as a means of community and family gathering. Through cooking good food, we nourish ourselves, and we nourish those around us: friends and family.

Translating these values within me to reality became more and more challenging as the years have passed. Owning my own business, working full time, tending to the house and yard, let alone thinking about children and dogs (our dog is really our first child), certainly does not lend much time to spend in the kitchen creating elaborate meals. I have found that when I get home at night and I'm hungry, I want to eat and I don't want to wait!

Thus, I created A Salad Soiree. This recipe book is filled with simple and easy recipes for anyone and everyone to create. They are fast and easy as well as nourishing and healthy. They are simple enough for a quiet evening at home and elaborate enough for entertaining. Often times these were thrown together from whatever ingredients were available in the refrigerator and the cupboard in a desperate attempt to feed a hungry tummy. Occasionally they were created in my head as I drove home thinking about what I could possibly make in the limited amount of time I had before the next activity. I chose to focus on salads for this book, simply because a salad is always my very favorite meal, any time of day. From the very basic green salad at dinner to the over-the-top production of a full blown five course salad meal, I just love salads! Most importantly though, all of the recipes were created for the pure enjoyment and appreciation of food; for I believe, that is what we all deserve.

"If you ate pasta and antipasto, would you still be hungry?"

~Anonymous~

Starters and Sides

Citrus Punch

6 c. mixed greens
2 small red tomatoes (Roma), sliced
2 small yellow tomatoes, sliced
1 small orange tomato, sliced
1 medium navel orange, sliced (peeled and pith removed, optional)
¼ c. fresh basil, coarsely chopped

Orange Basil Vinaigrette:
¼ c. fresh orange juice
¼ c. red wine vinegar
¼ c. extra virgin olive oil
1 Tbs. Dijon mustard
1 Tbs. fresh basil
1 clove garlic
Salt and pepper to taste

Slice all tomatoes evenly into small rounds, discarding end pieces. Slice the orange into rounds as well, discarding the two end slices on either side so that all slices are somewhat even in size. Remove any seeds from the oranges. (Navel oranges are generally seedless, but just in case, remove any that appear). Toss greens, tomatoes, oranges, and basil well.

Combine all vinaigrette ingredients and blend on high in a blender for 30 seconds. Just before serving, pour vinaigrette over salad mixture and toss very well to evenly coat. Be sure to present the salad with tomato slices of each color and orange slices visible on top.

Serves 6.

Dijon Potatoes

15-20 small new potatoes, quartered
1 c. Dijon vinaigrette***
½ red bell pepper, chopped into ¼ " squares
4 scallions, trimmed and chopped
8 oz. sharp white cheddar cheese, cubed into ¼" pieces
Salt and pepper to taste

***Your favorite store-bought vinaigrette is a perfect choice. My personal favorite is Maple Grove Farms of Vermont® Low-Fat Dijon Vinaigrette.

Bring 2 quarts of water to a boil. Wash and quarter the new potatoes. Boil until soft, but still somewhat firm (NOT too mushy). Drain and cool to room temperature.

Clean and chop red pepper and scallions. Cube the cheddar cheese. Mix all ingredients together in a large bowl, beautiful for presentation. Add salt and pepper to taste and continue to mix well until vinaigrette and all remaining ingredients are evenly distributed throughout the potato salad. Chill and serve.

Serves 4-6.

Fiery Red

This can be done on the grill with a grill basket or by roasting in the oven.

3 c. beets, chopped into ¼ - ½" pieces
2 c. sweet potatoes, chopped into ¼ - ½" pieces
1 c. carrots, chopped into ¼ - ½" pieces
1 red onion, chopped into ¼ - ½" pieces
½ c. grape seed or safflower oil
2 tsp. cayenne pepper
1 Tbs. fresh rosemary, finely diced
Salt and pepper

1 c. tamari roasted almonds, chopped (optional)**
1 c. sharp white cheddar cheese, shredded optional**

**When topped with nuts and cheese, the portion size may be doubled to serve as a main course meal or entrée.

Preheat grill to medium cooking heat.
Combine all ingredients (except those that are optional) and mix well to thoroughly coat with oil. Liberally salt and pepper for extra flavor.
Transfer mixture to a grill basket and grill on medium heat (charcoal or gas), stirring often until cooked well. Cook time will depend on each individual grill and grill temperature. All vegetables should be soft to the touch, while still maintaining their shape, and slightly browned with a "grilled" look.

To serve, top each individual serving dish with equal portions of roasted nuts and shredded cheese, if desired.

Serves 6. (**or 3 as a main course).

Dinner Flowers

6 c. mixed greens
1 head Bibb lettuce, washed, and spun
1 c. fresh nasturtiums (edible flowers)
2 Tbs. fresh herbs, chopped**

Citrus-Flower Vinaigrette:
¼ c. fresh orange juice
¼ c. red wine vinegar
¼ c. extra virgin olive oil
1 Tbs. Dijon mustard
1 Tbs. fresh basil
1 clove garlic, pressed
Salt and pepper to taste

**Any herb combination will suffice, depending upon personal preference.

Combine all salad ingredients and set aside. Blend all vinaigrette ingredients until smooth. Toss over salad.

Serves 4-6.

Fresh Mediterranean

6 c. fresh baby spinach
2 c. whole wheat fusilli (corkscrew) or penne regatta pasta
1 c. canned black olives, drained
2 cloves fresh garlic
1 large tomato, cored
¼ c. extra virgin olive oil
1 Tbs. fresh basil, chopped
¼ tsp. sea salt
¼ tsp. black pepper
1 ½ c. grilled chicken breast (chopped)

Cook and drain pasta as directed. Cool.
In a food processor, combine olives, garlic, tomato, olive oil, basil, salt, and pepper. Blend until smooth. Combine spinach, pasta, and blended sauce (as well as chicken, if desired) and toss well. Season to taste with additional salt and pepper.

Serve slightly chilled or at room temperature.

Serves 4.

Grilled Vegetable

A grill basket really makes this recipe work well.

1 bunch asparagus, chopped into 2" lengths
2 c. carrots, halved and cut into 2" lengths
1 c. red cabbage, shredded and chopped
1 red onion, coarsely chopped
2 medium zucchini, halved and cut into 2" lengths
2 whole garlic cloves, crushed
½ - ¾ c. extra virgin olive oil
2 Tbs. fresh herbs (basil, thyme, rosemary, etc.), chopped
Salt and pepper

Preheat grill to medium cooking heat.
Combine all ingredients and mix well to thoroughly coat with oil. Liberally salt and pepper for extra flavor. Transfer mixture to a grill basket and grill on medium heat (charcoal or gas), stirring often until cooked well. Cook time will depend on each individual grill and grill temperature. All vegetables should be soft to the touch and slightly browned with a "grilled" look.

Serves 4-6.

Fantastic Feta

This is a wonderfully flavorful salad for all times of the year. Goat feta works well with this salad, providing an extra bite. Cow feta can be substituted if necessary. Because pomegranates are seasonal, dried cranberries can be used alternatively. Finally, this salad requires only a drizzling of olive oil, as not to mask the robust flavors of the feta and roasted pepitas.

4-5 c. fresh arugula
1 c. crumbled goat feta
1 c. Ume Roasted Pepitas
½ - ¾ c. fresh pomegranate seeds or dried cranberries (optional)
2 Tbs. extra virgin olive oil

Ume Roasted Pepitas:
**These roasted seeds alone are one of my favorite snacks!
1 c. raw pepitas (pumpkin seeds)
1 Tbs. Ume Plum vinegar

Preheat oven to 350° F. Evenly spread seeds in glass or ceramic baking dish. Roast 10 minutes. Stir well and roast for an additional 10 minutes. Stir again and roast for final five minutes. Upon removing from oven, immediately add 1 Tbs. Ume Plum vinegar to evenly toss among and coat all seeds. Cool.

Combine all salad ingredients and drizzle with olive oil. Lightly toss to evenly coat.

Serves 4.

Grapefruit Avocado Dijon

2 ripe avocados, peeled and sliced
2 pink grapefruit, peeled and sectioned**
1 head Bibb lettuce
4 scallions, trimmed and chopped finely
4 large strawberries, washed and sliced

Dijon Vinaigrette:
¼ c. fresh grapefruit juice
¼ c. extra virgin olive oil
1 Tbs. lemon juice
1 Tbs. Dijon mustard
1 tsp. salt or to taste

Slice avocados and set aside. Before peeling grapefruit, boil hot water to carefully pour over the fruit and allow to cool. Then peel. (The hot water will help to remove the white skin and pith from underneath the peel.)
**Using a very sharp knife, carefully slice the grapefruit into sections, removing any remaining white skin. Wash and break lettuce to a reasonable fork size. Gently mix all salad ingredients (including scallions and strawberries) together. Set aside.

Combine all vinaigrette ingredients and mix well. Lightly drizzle over salad to the desired coating (not too much to make things soggy).

Serves 4-6.

Holiday Greens

1 Tbs. chopped fresh rosemary
2 tsp. olive oil
3 garlic cloves, unpeeled and crushed
1 ½ lbs. peeled sweet-potato, cut into ¾" pieces
2 c. orange sections (about 4 small oranges) ***
½ c. vertically sliced red onion
3 Tbs. pine nuts, toasted
1 6-oz bag pre-washed baby spinach

Vinaigrette:
3 Tbs. fresh orange juice
2 Tbs. olive oil
1 Tbs. stone ground mustard
1 Tbs. rice vinegar
1 Tbs. honey
¼ tsp. salt
¼ tsp. freshly ground black pepper
1 garlic clove, minced

**Blood oranges are ideal for the extra color and added flavor. Use whatever oranges are in season for best results.

Preheat oven to 400° F.
To prepare salad, combine first 4 ingredients, tossing well. Place potato mixture onto an oiled pan. Bake at 400° for 40 minutes, stirring occasionally. Remove from oven, cool. Discard garlic. Combine potato mixture, orange sections, onion, pine nuts, and spinach in a large bowl.

To prepare dressing, combine orange juice and remaining ingredients in blender or shaker. Drizzle dressing over salad, toss gently to coat.

Serves 4-6.

The Native

2 c. fresh or frozen corn kernels, thawed
1 bunch fresh asparagus, chopped into 1" lengths
½ c. extra virgin olive oil
1 c. sun-dried tomatoes, drained and thinly sliced
¼ tsp. sea salt
Pepper to taste

Preheat oven to 425° F.
Combine corn, asparagus, and olive oil in a glass baking dish or roasting pan. Stirring every 10-15 minutes, roast vegetables until they begin to show hints of a browned, roasted look, approximately 40 minutes. Remove from oven. Cool slightly. Add remaining ingredients and toss well.

Avocado and/or grilled chicken or fish can be added to make this a complete protein or a main course meal.

Serves 4-6.

Pico de Gallo

This salad is perfect for a hot summer day… "cool as a cucumber!"

2 large cucumbers
6 medium tomatoes
½ c. cilantro, diced
6 green onions, chopped
2 cloves garlic, pressed
½ c. extra virgin olive oil
½ c. white wine vinegar or champagne vinegar
1 tsp. salt
2/3 c. Cotija cheese, crumbled***

**Feta cheese can be used if Cotija is unavailable.

Wash and peel cucumbers. Quarter and then chop into 1" pie shaped pieces. Wash tomatoes and remove seeds to chop into similar size pieces as the cucumber. Mix all ingredients together, except the cheese. Coat with the oil. Marinate at room temperature for 1 hour. Sprinkle cheese on top and lightly stir for presentation.

Serves 6.

Rasparagus

6 c. mixed greens
1 lb. fresh asparagus, washed and trimmed of the ends
1 Tbs. extra virgin olive oil
1 pint fresh raspberries, washed
¼ c. pecans, chopped
1 Tbs. sugar or Stevia (to candy the pecans)
Optional: ½ c. Feta or Bleu cheese

Raspberry Vinaigrette:
¼ c. balsamic vinegar
¼ c. raspberry vinegar (red wine or champagne will work, if necessary)
¼ c. extra virgin olive oil
2 Tbs. water
1 Tbs. Dijon mustard
1 clove garlic
Salt and pepper to taste

Pre-heat oven to a broil.
Drizzle extra virgin olive oil over the asparagus and broil (stirring often) for 10-12 minutes. Remove and cool to room temperature. Heat sugar or Stevia in a skillet until very hot. Add pecans and stir constantly until fully coated and "candied." Cool. Mix all salad ingredients together in a large bowl, beautiful for presentation.

Blend all vinaigrette ingredients in a blender until fully emulsified. Pour over salad and toss well, careful not to break the fragile raspberries.

**Feta or Bleu cheese can be added to top the salad at the very end for those who fancy something with more of a bite and tang than just the raspberries.

Serves 4-6.

Sweet and Tangy Mediterranean

4 c. cooked brown or green lentils, rinsed and drained
1 c. dried cranberries
1 c. feta cheese, crumbled
½ red onion, sliced thinly
1-1½ c. balsamic vinaigrette
1 Tbs. Dijon mustard (optional**)
½ c. walnuts, chopped (optional)
½ tsp. salt

1 6-oz bag pre-washed baby spinach

***The Dijon mustard can be added to the vinaigrette to add a little bit of an **extra** bite. The feta adds a bite in and of itself.*

Combine lentils, cranberries, feta, onion and vinaigrette. Toss well. Use enough vinaigrette to evenly coat all ingredients. Divide the spinach evenly on to the 6-8 serving plates. Top with a generous amount of lentil salad. Sprinkle with chopped walnuts if desired.

Serves 6-8.

"A nickel will get you on the subway, but garlic will get you a seat."
~Old New York Proverb~

Main Meals

Citrus Basil Fish

6 c. mixed greens
1 c. shredded carrots
3 scallions, chopped
2 lbs. fresh fish (halibut or swordfish)

Orange Basil Vinaigrette:
½ c. fresh orange juice
¼ c. red wine vinegar
¼ c. extra virgin olive oil
1 Tbs. Dijon mustard
1 Tbs. fresh basil
1 clove garlic
Salt and pepper to taste

Orange Basil Salsa:
2 navel oranges, separated and diced
1 large tomato, cored and diced
1 scallion, chopped
1 Tbs. fresh basil, minced
1 clove garlic, pressed
1 Tbs. lime juice
2 tsp. extra virgin olive oil
1 jalapeño, seeded and minced (wear gloves)

Preparation:
Combine all vinaigrette ingredients and divide in half. Combine one half of mixture with fish to marinate 4-6 hours or overnight. Pre-heat grill to low-medium heat. Grill fish on low heat evenly until thoroughly cooked. Cool to room temperature and divide into 4-6 servings.

Combine all salsa ingredients and chill for 4-6 hours to allow flavors to develop.

Combine fresh greens with carrots, scallions, and remaining vinaigrette. Toss well. Center each plate with 1 cup of the green mixture. Top each salad mixture with 3-4 oz. grilled fish and ¼ c. Orange Basil Salsa. Enjoy.

Serves 4-6.

Everything But the Kitchen Sink

6 c. mixed greens
1 large carrot, shredded
2 mushrooms, sliced
3 Roma tomatoes, sliced
1 c. cauliflower, chopped
1 c. broccoli, chopped (optional-not everyone likes the bitter taste of raw broccoli)
1 large beet, shredded
1 c. sunflower sprouts
3 scallions, diced
½-¾ c. walnuts, chopped
1 Tbs. fresh basil, chopped

Walnut Vinaigrette:
¼ c. walnut oil
¼ c. red wine or champagne vinegar
1 Tbs. Dijon mustard
1 tsp. fresh basil, chopped
1 tsp. garlic, pressed
Salt and pepper

Combine all salad ingredients and set aside. Blend all vinaigrette ingredients until smooth.
Toss vinaigrette into salad. Be sure to evenly coat all elements.

Serves 4-6.

Island Beef

2 lbs. flank steak, thinly sliced
½ c. soy sauce or tamari
¼ c. honey
¼ c. water
¼ c. rice vinegar
2 tsp. crushed garlic
2 tsp. peeled and crushed ginger root
2 scallions, chopped

6 c. Romaine lettuce

Island Salsa:
2 c. diced pineapple
1 c. diced red bell pepper
½ c. diced red onion
1 tsp. minced or crushed garlic
1 small Serrano pepper, cored and minced
1 tsp. rice vinegar
Salt to taste

Preparation:
In a medium sauce pan, combine soy sauce, honey, water, vinegar, garlic and ginger. Heat until honey is melted and mixed well. Remove from heat and cool. Transfer to gallon size plastic bag and add flank steak. Allow to marinade in refrigerator for 6-8 hours, shaking bag occasionally to evenly disperse marinade.

Combine all salsa ingredients and chill for 4-6 hours to allow flavors to develop. Preheat grill to medium heat. Remove steak from marinade and boil remaining liquid for further use. Cook steaks 5-7 minutes on each side, or until thoroughly cooked, occasionally basting with the boiled, reserved marinade. Allow to cool.

Toss steak and any remaining boiled marinade (cooled) with the Romaine lettuce leaves. Serve topped with generous portions of the Island Salsa.

Serves 4-6.

Pure Energy

2 whole avocados, chopped
2 small tomatoes, chopped
1 yellow bell pepper, seeded and chopped
1 c. mushrooms, sliced
1 c. raw carrots, chopped
1 head romaine lettuce, coarsely chopped
½ c. raw sunflower seeds
¼ c. crumbled dulse (optional)

Vinaigrette:
¼ c. extra virgin olive oil
¼ c. apple cider vinegar
2 Tbs. lemon juice
Salt and pepper

Chop all salad ingredients into ½" pieces and mix well with vinaigrette. Serve chilled.

Serves 3-4.

"Rawsta" Fresca

This is just perfectly refreshing on a hot summer day!

Spiralized "Rawsta":
2 large carrots
2 large zucchini

Tomato Sauce:
1 large red Heirloom tomato
½ shallot
8 leaves fresh basil
¼ tsp. sea salt
1 large yellow tomato, chopped
4 leaves fresh basil, chopped
1 Tbs. extra virgin olive oil
2 tsp. red wine vinegar
1 tsp. red pepper flakes

Using a food spiralizer or garnisher really works best to create the spaghetti-like ribbons or noodles. However, a simple vegetable peeler can be used to create linguini-like noodles instead.

Spiralize carrots and zucchini and set aside.

Combine red tomato, shallot, basil, and salt in food processor. Blend well. Add chopped yellow tomato, remaining basil, olive oil, vinegar, and red pepper flakes and stir well. Refrigerate mixture for about 4 hours to allow flavors to develop. To serve: toss carrots and zucchini together and pour tomato sauce evenly over "rawsta."
Enjoy.

Grilled chicken or fish can be added for protein to complete this salad as a main meal.

Serves 2-4.

Shining Mountain Waldorf

6 c. mixed greens
1 c. red grapes, halved
1 c. green apple, chopped
1 c. walnuts, chopped
1 c. goat feta, crumbled

Mustard Vinaigrette:
¼ c. extra virgin olive oil
¼ c. balsamic vinegar
1 Tbs. Dijon mustard
1 tsp. fresh basil, chopped
1 small shallot, minced
Salt and pepper

Combine all salad ingredients and set aside. Blend all vinaigrette ingredients until smooth. Toss vinaigrette into salad. Be sure to evenly coat all elements.

Grilled chicken, chopped, can be added to this if desired.

Serves 4-6.

Simple Grilled Chicken

6 c. mixed greens
1 large carrot, shredded
2 mushrooms, sliced
3 Roma tomatoes, sliced

Chicken:
4-6 (2 lbs. total) boneless, skinless chicken breasts, rinsed and trimmed

Marinade:
¼ c. Bragg's Liquid Aminos, tamari, or soy sauce
¼ c. lemon juice
1 Tbs. dried Herbs de Provence

½ c. Italian vinaigrette**
**Your favorite store-bought brand works well. To make the dressing homemade:
¼ c. extra virgin olive oil
¼ c. red wine vinegar
1 Tbs. lemon juice
1 tsp. Herbs de Provence
Salt and pepper

Preparation:
Combine all marinade ingredients for the chicken and add chicken to marinate refrigerated 4-6 hours or overnight. Grill chicken on low heat evenly until thoroughly cooked. Cool to room temperature.

Combine all salad ingredients and toss with vinaigrette.

Slice chicken breasts and serve atop salad mixture.

Serves 4-6.

Spicy Peach Chicken

6 c. mixed greens
½ red onion, halved and sliced thinly

Chicken:
4-6 (2 lbs. total) boneless, skinless chicken breasts, rinsed and trimmed
Marinade-
¼ c. red wine vinegar
1 Tbs. Dijon mustard
¼ c. lemon juice
1 Tbs. fresh ginger juice
1 Tbs. fresh oregano, chopped

Peach Salsa:
2 large ripe peaches, chopped into ½" pieces
¼ c. red onion, sliced and finely chopped
2 Tbs. fresh oregano, chopped
2 Tbs. red wine vinegar
1 clove garlic, pressed
1 Tbs. fresh ginger juice

Preparation:
Combine all marinade ingredients and add chicken to marinate 4-6 hours or overnight. Grill chicken on low heat evenly until thoroughly cooked. Cool to room temperature.

Combine all salsa ingredients and chill for 4-6 hours to allow flavors to develop.

Combine fresh greens with the red onion and toss well.

Center each plate with 1 cup of the green mixture. Top each salad mixture with one grilled chicken breast and at least ¼ c. Peach Salsa. Enjoy.

Serves 4-6.

"STRESSED is DESSERTS spelled backwords."
                                              ~Anonymous~

*For those of us that prefer to wake up on
"The Sweeter Side,"
any of these recipes can be used for tasty breakfast ideas
as well.*

The Sweeter Side

Berry Fruity

3 c. fresh strawberries, halved
2 c. fresh blueberries
1 c. fresh raspberries
1 c. fresh blackberries or boysenberries
1 large pear, diced
½ c. slivered almonds

2 Tbs. honey
1 tsp. lemon juice
½ tsp. vanilla

Fresh mint leaves (optional)

Combine all fruit and nuts into a large bowl. Combine honey, lemon juice and vanilla in a microwave safe container. Microwave on high for 10-15 seconds, until honey begins to liquify. Drizzle honey mixture over the fruit and toss lightly. Top with fresh mint leaves. Chill to serve.

Serves 4-6.

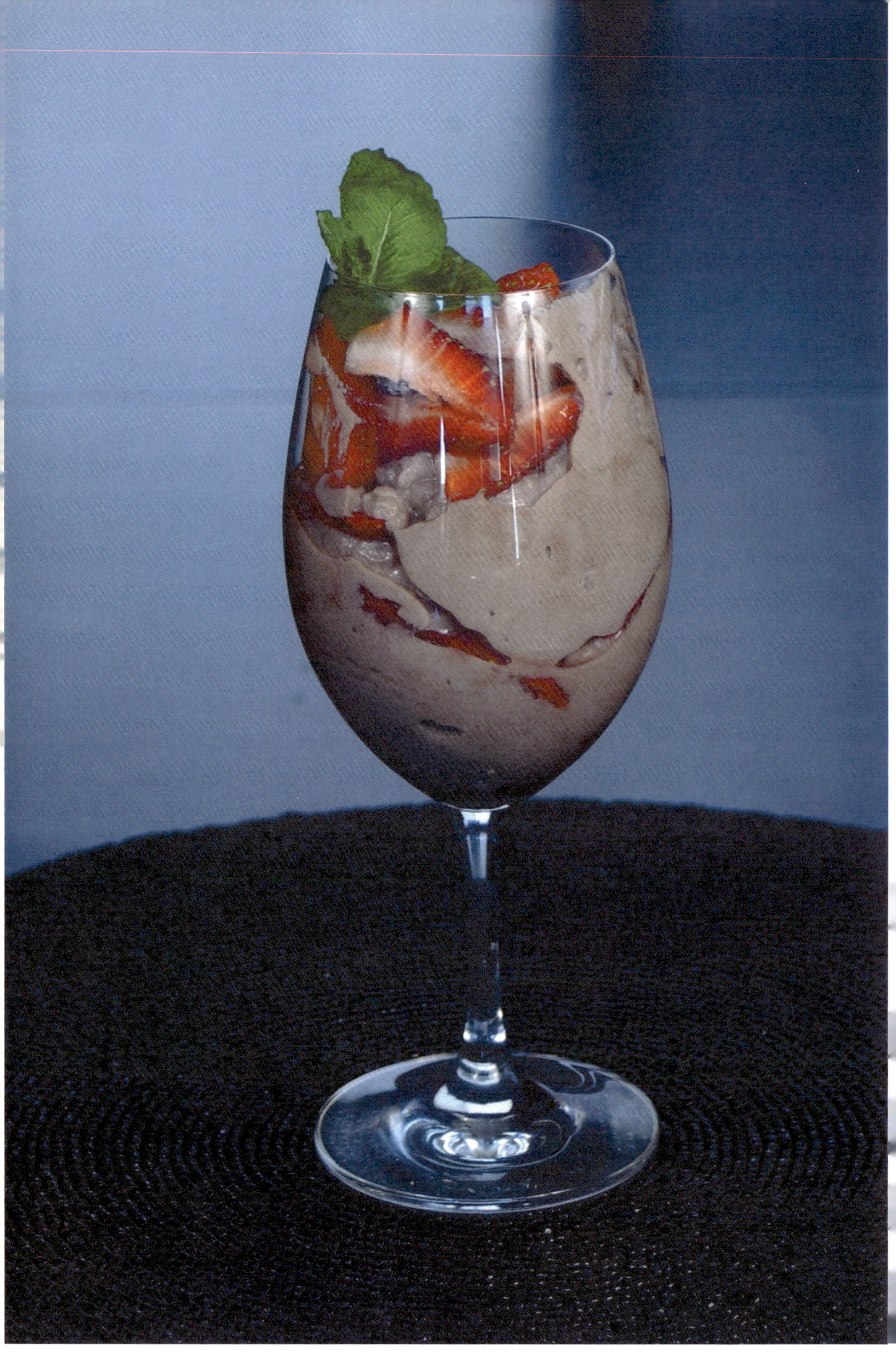

Strawberry Ricotta

4 c. low fat ricotta cheese
1 c. fresh strawberries
1 Tbs. cocoa powder
½ c. raw honey
½ c. slivered almonds

Add honey and cocoa to a microwave safe bowl and heat on high for 20 seconds, until honey becomes smooth. Pour honey and cocoa mixture into ricotta and stir well until cocoa is evenly mixed.
Chill for several hours.
Wash and slice strawberries. Divide ricotta into serving bowls and top with strawberries and almonds. Garnish with fresh mint if desired.

Serves 4-6.

Muesli Fruit

4 c. yogurt (plain or flavored)** (NOT non-fat)
1 ½ c. raw oats
1 c. fresh strawberries, chopped
1 c. fresh blueberries
1 c. chopped apples
1 c. walnuts or almonds, chopped
½ - ¾ c. raw honey***
2 tsp. cinnamon
1 tsp. vanilla

**Plain yogurt will yield a richer, whole taste, preferable for morning meals. Using flavored yogurt will lead to a much sweeter blend which can be used for desserts.

***Sweeten for personal preference.

Combine all ingredients and mix well. Chill overnight to allow oats to soften and sweetness/flavor to fully develop.

Serves 4-6.

Winter Wheat Berry

2 ½ c. raw wheat berries, rinsed
4 c. boiling water
2 c. red and green grapes, halved
1 c. dried cranberries
1 c. chopped apples
1 c. walnuts, chopped
½ c. walnut oil
½ c. raw honey
2 Tbs. lemon juice
1 tsp. cinnamon
1 tsp. vanilla
¼ c. fresh mint, minced

Preparation:
In a large bowl or saucepan, pour boiling water over the wheat berries and cover. Let sit 8 hours or overnight. Rinse and drain of any excess water. The wheat berries should be slightly chewy and maintain their shape.
Combine walnut oil, honey, lemon juice, cinnamon, and vanilla. While adding fruit, walnuts, and mint, evenly pour honey mixture over fruit and wheat berry mixture. Continue to stir well until evenly coated.

Serves 4-6.

"Do vegetarians eat animal crackers?"
~Anonymous~

ENJOY!